# THE BURGER BOOK

Edited by
Norma Miller

OCTOPUS

# Contents

**This edition first published 1979 by
Octopus Books Limited
59 Grosvenor Street, London W1**

Reprinted 1981

© 1979 Octopus Books Limited

ISBN 0 7064 1011 4

Produced by Mandarin Publishers Ltd
22a Westlands Road,
Quarry Bay, Hong Kong
Printed in Hong Kong

*Frontispiece:* LOW CALORIE LAMB BURGER *(page 23)*
*(Photograph: Outline Slimming Bureau)*

# Weights and Measures

All measurements in this book are based on Imperial weights and measures, with American equivalents given in parenthesis.

Measurements in *weight* in the Imperial and American system are the same. Liquid measurements are different, and the following table shows the equivalents:

### Liquid measurements
| | |
|---|---|
| 1 Imperial pint | 20 fluid ounces |
| 1 American pint | 16 fluid ounces |
| 1 American cup | 8 fluid ounces |

Level spoon measurements are used in all the recipes.

### Spoon measurements
| | |
|---|---|
| 1 tablespoon (1T) | 15 ml |
| 1 teaspoon | 5 ml |

# INTRODUCTION

Burgers are not just a round of meat in a buttered bun. They can be made using fish as the basic ingredient, and almost any kind of meat, ranging from beef through to veal and pork. Different toppings and sauces, French fries and crisp salads, turn a burger from a simple snack into a filling meal.

The basic burger (meat, onion, egg and seasoning) can be varied using all kinds of flavourings such as herbs, spices, vegetables and fruit. Burgers are quick and simple to prepare, making them an ideal family meal. Always use good quality, freshly ground meat. (It is advisable to deal only with suppliers whose standards of quality and hygiene you know to be completely reliable.) The ground meat, or flaked fish, can be mixed with a wide variety of ingredients, including leftovers like egg yolks, cooked rice and creamed potato. A pound of ground meat combined with creamed potato will make sufficient quantity for six people (allowing one burger each). By combining different ingredients in this way it is possible to produce a very economical meal, which is nourishing and full of flavour.

For grilling (broiling): brush the grill tray with oil and preheat. Add the burgers, brush with oil and brown quickly on both sides. Reduce the heat and continue grilling, turning occasionally, until the burgers are cooked to your liking. Grilled (broiled) burgers take about 10 minutes.

For frying: heat sufficient oil in a frying pan (skillet) for shallow frying. When hot, carefully slide in the burgers and fry, turning occasionally. Fried burgers take about 10 minutes.

For barbecuing: first of all remember to light the fire about 30 to 45 minutes before needed, so the flames die down and the embers are glowing, ready for cooking. Preheat the barbecue grid: this gives the characteristic 'ring' marks to barbecued food. Place the burgers on the grid, brown, then turn and cook until done to your liking. While they are cooking, brush them with your favourite barbecue sauce. Barbecued burgers take about 10 minutes to cook. If the grid is widely spaced it is better to cook on a flat solid surface, otherwise the burgers have a tendency to fall into the fire! Remember to cook any burgers containing pork all the way through.

Homemade burgers can be successfully frozen, although they should not be too highly seasoned or spiced.

To freeze: open (flash) freeze on a tray until solid, then wrap each burger individually in foil and pack together in a freezer bag. Seal the bag and return it to the freezer. Freeze for up to three months.

To thaw: take the burgers out as and when required. Fry them from frozen in shallow fat or oil until cooked through – about 10 minutes on each side.

SALAD BURGERS *(page 11)*
*(Photograph: Home Baking Bureau)*

8

# BEEF BURGERS

## Basic Beef Burger

1 onion, grated
1 lb. minced (ground) beef
1 egg
salt and pepper

1 teaspoon Worcestershire sauce
pinch of dried mixed herbs
1 tablespoon oil

Mix together the onion, beef, egg, seasoning, Worcestershire sauce
and herbs. Divide into four or eight portions and shape into large or
small burgers. Brush with the oil and grill (broil) for 3-6 minutes on
each side.
**Serves 4**


## Beef Burger Bean Pasties

1 tablespoon oil
4 beefburgers (see above)
2 tablespoons dried onions,
  reconstituted
8 oz. can baked beans

1 teaspoon tomato purée (paste)
salt and pepper
13 oz. packet frozen shortcrust
  (pie) pastry, thawed
beaten egg, to glaze

Heat the oil in a frying pan (skillet) and fry the beefburgers until
cooked. Drain and cool. Mix together the onion, beans, tomato
purée (paste) and seasoning. Roll out the dough and cut out four
7 inch circles. Place a beefburger on top of each dough circle and
spoon over the bean mixture. Dampen the dough edges and draw up
over the filling. Pinch the edges together to seal. Brush with the
beaten egg and bake in a moderately hot oven, 400°F, Gas Mark 6 for
25-30 minutes, or until the pastry is golden brown.
**Serves 4**

# Burger Roll

1 ½ lb. minced (ground) beef
3 oz. (1 ½ cups) fresh breadcrumbs
2 eggs, beaten
2 teaspoons dry mustard
salt and pepper

1 onion, finely chopped
2 tablespoons chopped parsley
¼ oz. (1 T) flour
4 oz. (1 cup) cheese, grated
1 oz. (2 T) butter, melted

Mix together the beef, breadcrumbs, eggs, mustard, seasoning, onion and parsley. Sprinkle the flour onto a rectangle of foil, 10 × 15 inches, and spread the meat mixture over thickly, almost to the edges. Chill thoroughly.

Cover the meat with the cheese and roll up, starting at the narrow end and using the foil to lift the meat. Place on a baking sheet with the join underneath. Brush with the melted butter and bake in a moderate oven, 350°F, Gas Mark 4 for 1 hour. Cut into four slices and serve with chips (French fries).
**Serves 4**


# Salad Burgers

1 packet soft bread roll mix or 8
  hamburger buns
1 ½ lb. minced (ground) beef
1 onion, chopped
pinch of dried thyme
pinch of chopped parsley
salt and pepper
1-2 eggs
oil

2 onions, sliced into rings
¼ oz. (1 T) flour
tomato ketchup
**Accompaniments:**
green salad
coleslaw
tomatoes
parsley
French dressing

Make up the bread roll mix, according to packet instructions. Shape into rolls, bake and cool. Combine the beef, onion, herbs and seasoning with enough egg to bind. Divide into eight portions and shape into burgers. Heat oil in a frying pan (skillet) and fry the burgers until cooked. Remove from the pan and keep hot. Coat the onion rings in the flour and fry until crisp.

Cut the bread rolls or buns in half and place a burger in each with a few onion rings. Spread over a little ketchup and serve with the accompaniments.
**Makes 8**

# Chilli Billy Buns

1 tablespoon oil
1 onion, chopped
8 oz. minced (ground) beef
1 small can baked beans
1 tablespoon chilli seasoning

salt and pepper
4 rolls (buns)
tomato wedges and watercress to
  garnish

Heat the oil in a frying pan (skillet) and fry the onion for 3 minutes.
Add the beef and cook, stirring occasionally, for 10 minutes. Add the
beans and seasonings. Bring to the boil, reduce the heat and simmer
for 10 minutes.
   Meanwhile, slit the rolls (buns) in half and toast on both sides.
Divide the meat mixture between the rolls (buns) and garnish with
tomato wedges and watercress.
**Serves 4**

# Crispy Burgers

1 lb. minced (ground) beef
2 oz. dry beef and onion soup mix
2 oz. (⅓ cup) sultanas (seedless
  white raisins)
salt and pepper

4 tablespoons (¼ cup) water
8 large slices of white bread, crusts
  removed
1 tablespoon oil

Mix together the beef, soup powder, sultanas (seedless white raisins),
seasoning and water. Divide into eight portions and shape into
'sausages'. Place a 'sausage' in the centre of each slice of bread and
bring the bread sides together to enclose the 'sausage'. Place on a
baking sheet with the joins underneath. Brush liberally with the oil
and bake in a moderate oven, 350°F, Gas Mark 4 until the bread is
crisp and golden. Serve hot with brown or tomato sauce.
**Serves 4**

BASIC BEEF BURGERS *(page 10)*
*(Photograph: British Meat Promotion Executive)*

# Beef Burgers in Blue Cheese Sauce

1 lb. minced (ground) beef
1 egg
1 onion, finely chopped
1 garlic clove, crushed
½ teaspoon salt
1 teaspoon chopped parsley
½ teaspoon dried mixed herbs
½ teaspoon dried basil
¼ teaspoon dry mustard
1 tablespoon Worcestershire sauce
1 oz. (2 T) butter
**Sauce:**
2 oz. (¼ cup) butter
2 oz. (½ cup) flour
1 pint (2½ cups) milk
½ teaspoon salt
4 oz. (1 cup) blue cheese, crumbled

Put the beef, egg, onion, garlic, salt, parsley, herbs, mustard and Worcestershire sauce in a bowl and mix well together. Form into eight burgers. Melt the butter in a frying pan (skillet) and fry the burgers for 3–4 minutes on each side. Keep warm.

To make the sauce, melt the butter in a saucepan and add the flour. Cook for 1 minute, stirring continuously, then gradually add the milk. Bring to the boil and add the salt. Cook for 2–3 minutes, then remove from the heat and stir in the cheese.

Arrange the burgers in an ovenproof dish and pour over the sauce. Bake in a hot oven, 425°F, Gas Mark 7 for 20 minutes.
**Serves 4**

# Beef-and-bacon Burgers

1½ lb. minced (ground) beef
1 onion, finely chopped
2 bacon rashers (slices), chopped
1 tablespoon Worcestershire sauce
2 oz. (1 cup) fresh breadcrumbs
1 small egg
salt and pepper
½ oz. (2 T) flour
oil for frying

Thoroughly mix together all the ingredients, except the flour and oil. Form into four to six burgers and coat with the flour. Fry the burgers in hot oil for 7–10 minutes on each side. Serve hot in toasted rolls (buns).
**Serves 4-6**

# Prune Burgers

1 lb. minced (ground) beef
2 oz. (1 cup) fresh breadcrumbs
1 teaspoon dried mixed herbs
10 prunes, soaked overnight
¾ pint (2 cups) lager

½ oz. (2 T) flour
4 tablespoons (¼ cup) tomato
  purée (paste)
salt and pepper
1 tablespoon oil

Mix together the beef, breadcrumbs and mixed herbs and shape into eight small burgers. Put the remaining ingredients, except the oil, in the saucepan and, stirring continuously, bring to the boil. Cover and simmer for 50 minutes.

Ten minutes before the sauce is ready, brush the burgers with the oil and grill (broil) until cooked. Serve hot with the prune sauce.
**Serves 4**

# Curried Burgers

1 lb. minced (ground) beef
2 tablespoons fresh breadcrumbs
1 small egg
1 large onion, chopped
1 teaspoon chilli powder
salt and pepper
3 tablespoons oil

1 large cooking apple, peeled, cored
  and sliced
1 tablespoon mild curry powder
¼ oz. (1 T) flour
1 pint (2½ cups) stock
1 tablespoon mango chutney

Mix together the beef, breadcrumbs, egg, half the onion, the chilli powder and seasoning. Shape into four burgers and grill (broil) for 2-3 minutes on each side.

Heat the oil and fry the remaining onion and the apple until soft. Stir in the curry powder and cook for a further 2-3 minutes. Add the remaining ingredients and bring to the boil, stirring continuously. Add the burgers and cook for 15 minutes. Serve with rice.
**Serves 4**

# Spicy Burgers

1 lb. minced (ground) beef
2 oz. (1 cup) fresh breadcrumbs
2 teaspoons chilli seasoning
2 onions, chopped

1 teaspoon black pepper
2 teaspoons tomato purée (paste)
½ teaspoon garlic powder

Put all the ingredients in a bowl and mix together thoroughly. Flour your hands and shape the mixture into six burgers. Grill (broil) for 3-4 minutes on each side. Serve with chips (French fries), beans and onion relish.
**Makes 6**

# Jumbo Burgers

2 lb. minced (ground) beef
2 onions, finely chopped
salt and pepper

1 egg, beaten
1 tablespoon oil

Mix together the beef, onions and seasoning. Bind with the egg and turn the mixture onto a floured surface. Divide into eight portions and shape into burgers. Brush with the oil and grill (broil) for 8-10 minutes, turning frequently. Serve in a roll (bun).
**Makes 8**

# Tomato Burgers

12 oz. (1½ cups) minced (ground) beef
3 tablespoons fresh breadcrumbs
2 carrots, grated
1 onion, chopped

2 teaspoons tomato purée (paste)
½ teaspoon garlic powder
1 teaspoon dried marjoram
½ teaspoon cayenne pepper
salt and pepper

Mix all the ingredients thoroughly together. Flour your hands and shape the meat mixture into four burgers. Grill (broil) until cooked.
**Serves 4**

SPICY BURGERS
(Photograph: Crosse & Blackwell)

# Onion Burgers

1 lb. minced (ground) beef
2 oz. (1 cup) fresh breadcrumbs
1 small onion, grated
1 egg, beaten
salt and pepper
3 tablespoons oil
1 large onion, sliced

4 oz. (1 cup) mushrooms, sliced
¼ oz. (1 T) flour
½ pint (1 ¼ cups) stock
1 tablespoon tomato purée (paste)
2 oz. (1 cup) shell-shaped noodles,
  cooked and kept hot

Mix together the beef, half the breadcrumbs, the grated onion, egg
and seasoning. Form into eight burgers and coat with the remaining
breadcrumbs. Fry in the oil in a frying pan (skillet) for 15 minutes,
then place in a casserole.

Stir the sliced onion and mushrooms into the oil remaining in the
frying pan (skillet) and fry for 2-3 minutes. Sprinkle over the flour,
then stir in the stock and tomato purée (paste). Bring to the boil,
stirring, and pour over the burgers in the casserole. Bake in a
moderate oven, 350°F, Gas Mark 4 for 30 minutes. Serve with the
noodles.
**Serves 4**

# LAMB BURGERS

## Lamb Burgers

1 large onion, grated
1 oz. (2 T) butter
1 lb. minced (ground) lamb
½ small pepper, cored, seeded and
  finely diced
1 tablespoon tomato purée (paste)

1 teaspoon dried marjoram
1 teaspoon dried thyme
salt and pepper
3 oz. (1½ cups) fresh breadcrumbs
1 teaspoon clear honey

Fry the onion in the butter until softened, then mix thoroughly with
all the remaining ingredients. Divide into eight portions and shape
into burgers. Grill (broil) for 5 minutes on each side.
**Makes 8**

## Minty Lamb Burgers

1 lb. minced (ground) lamb
1 onion, finely chopped
1 tablespoon chopped fresh mint
½ teaspoon salt
¼ teaspoon pepper

1 egg
oil for frying
4 soft rolls (buns)
4 tomatoes, sliced

Mix together the lamb, onion, mint and seasoning, and bind with the
egg. Form into eight burgers and fry in the oil. Split the rolls (buns)
in half and toast the cut sides. Place a lamb burger on each half and
top with sliced tomatoes. Serve with salad.
**Makes 8**

# Herby Spiced Lamb Burgers

1 lb. minced (ground) lamb
2 tablespoons fresh breadcrumbs
1 teaspoon chopped fresh rosemary
1 onion, grated
salt and pepper

1 tablespoon blackcurrant syrup
**Garnish:**
tomato slices
lettuce leaves

Mix all the ingredients together. Turn onto a floured board and knead. Shape into four burgers. Grill (broil) until cooked. Serve in floury baps (buns), garnished with tomato slices and lettuce.
**Serves 4**

# Lamb and Veal Burgers

8 oz. boneless lamb, minced
  (ground) twice
8 oz. boneless veal, minced
  (ground) twice
2 tablespoons fresh breadcrumbs

1 onion, grated
1 tablespoon orange juice
1 teaspoon dried mixed herbs
¼ teaspoon grated nutmeg
salt and pepper

Mix all the ingredients together. Turn onto a floured surface and shape into four burgers. Grill (broil) until golden. Serve with a green vegetable, tomatoes, mushrooms and chips (French fries).
**Serves 4**

# Lamb Burgers with Orange

1 lb. boneless lamb, minced
  (ground) twice
2 tablespoons fresh breadcrumbs
1 tablespoon orange juice

1 onion, grated
1 teaspoon chopped fresh sage
salt and pepper
orange slices to garnish

Mix all the ingredients together. Turn onto a floured surface and shape into four burgers. Grill (broil) or fry until golden. Serve with a vegetable as a main meal, garnished with orange slices.
**Serves 4**

HERBY SPICED LAMB BURGERS, LAMB AND VEAL
BURGERS, LAMB BURGERS WITH ORANGE, LAMB
BURGERS WITH TOMATO SAUCE *(page 22)*
*(Photograph: Delrosa)*

# Lamb Burgers with Tomato Sauce

1 lb. minced (ground) lamb
1 onion, chopped
1 tablespoon chopped parsley
salt and pepper
¼ oz. (1 T) flour
parsley sprigs to garnish
**Tomato sauce:**
2 medium onions, finely chopped

1 garlic clove, crushed
1 oz. (2 T) butter
14 oz. can tomatoes, drained
1 tablespoon tomato purée (paste)
1 tablespoon rosehip syrup
1 teaspoon dried mixed herbs
pinch of grated nutmeg
salt and pepper

Prepare the sauce by frying the onions and garlic in the melted butter in a saucepan until softened. Stir in the tomatoes, tomato purée (paste), rosehip syrup, herbs, nutmeg and seasoning. Cover and simmer for 25 minutes.

Mix all the burger ingredients together and form into four burgers. Grill (broil) until cooked. Pour over the sauce, garnish with parsley and serve with grilled (broiled) mushrooms.
**Serves 4**

# Barbecued Lamb Burgers

4 lamb burgers (see page 19)
juice of 1 lemon
1 tablespoon Worcestershire sauce
salt and pepper
1 small red pepper, cored, seeded
  and finely chopped

2 bananas, finely chopped
4 small onions, finely chopped
4 mushrooms, finely chopped

Place the lamb burgers on a barbecue rack. Mix together the lemon
juice, Worcestershire sauce and seasoning in saucepan. Brush the
burgers with the sauce and cook on both sides. Meanwhile, add the
remaining ingredients to the sauce. Bring to the boil and cook for 5
minutes. Serve the sauce with the burgers.
**Serves 4**


# Low Calorie Lamb Burgers

12 oz. minced (ground) lamb
1 onion, chopped
½ oz. (¼ cup) low calorie fresh
  breadcrumbs
1 small egg
1 beef stock (bouillon) cube,
  crumbled
1 teaspoon dried mixed herbs
salt and pepper

1 oz. (2 T) low fat spread
**Filling:**
2 oz. (½ cup) mushrooms, sliced
1 tablespoon horseradish sauce
1 tomato, sliced
2 tablespoons grated cheese
**Garnish:**
tomato twists
parsley sprigs

Mix together the lamb, onion, breadcrumbs, egg, stock (bouillon)
cube, herbs and seasoning. Divide into eight portions and shape into
thin burgers. Melt the low fat spread and gently cook the burgers for
4-5 minutes on each side. Remove from the pan and drain.

Add the mushrooms to the remaining fat in the pan and fry for 1
minute. Mix with the horseradish and seasoning. Place a slice of
tomato on top of four of the burgers and top with the mushroom
mixture. Cover with the remaining burgers and sprinkle over the
cheese. Brown under the grill (broiler). Garnish with tomato twists
and parsley.
**Serves 4**

# Blue Burgers

4 lamb burgers (see page 19)
4 rolls (buns)
2 oz. (¼ cup) butter
1 teaspoon made mustard
4 oz. blue cheese

**Garnish:**
onion slices
tomato slices
gherkins (sweet dill pickles)

Grill (broil) the burgers until cooked and browned on both sides. Split the rolls (buns) and spread with the butter and mustard. Slice the cheese into four. To serve, place a hot burger in each roll (bun) and top with a portion of cheese. Close the roll (bun) tightly so that the warmth of the burger slightly melts the cheese. Garnish with the salad ingredients.
**Serves 4**

# Indian Burgers

2 oz. (¼ cup) butter
1 tablespoon garam masala
1 lb. minced (ground) lamb

3 tablespoons plain yogurt
½ teaspoon salt
3 tablespoons water

Melt half the butter in a frying pan (skillet). Add the garam masala and cook gently for 5 minutes. Place the meat, yogurt and salt in a mixing bowl and mix together thoroughly. Add the garam masala and mix well. Divide into 12 and shape into small burgers. Fry gently in the remaining butter until soft, taking care that they do not break. Turn occasionally and add the water. Cook until the water has evaporated. Serve with rice.
**Serves 4-6**

BLUE BURGER
*(Photograph: Danish Food Centre)*

# Pineapple Burgers

1 lb. minced (ground) lamb
1 small onion, chopped
2 tablespoons tomato ketchup
salt and pepper
1 egg, beaten
1 oz. (¼ cup) flour

2 tablespoons oil
8 canned pineapple rings
pineapple can syrup, made up to ¼
  pint (⅔ cup) with water
1 teaspoon cornflour (cornstarch)
  dissolved in 1 tablespoon water

Mix together the meat, onion, ketchup and seasoning and bind with the egg. Form into eight burgers. Coat with the flour mixed with salt and pepper, and fry in the hot oil for 10-15 minutes.

Place the pineapple rings and the syrup mixture in a saucepan and heat for 2 minutes. Place one ring on top of each burger. Thicken the syrup with the cornflour (cornstarch) and serve with the burgers.
**Serves 4**


# Apple Burgers

1 large potato, peeled and grated
1 lb. minced (ground) lamb
1 egg, beaten

1 onion, chopped
1 cooking apple, cored and grated
2 oz. (½ cup) flour

Squeeze the excess moisture out of the potato. Mix all the ingredients together and divide into four. Shape into burgers and fry or grill (broil) for 7 minutes on each side. Drain well before serving, if fried.
**Serves 4**

# Giant Pasta Burger

1 lb. minced (ground) lamb
1 onion, grated
salt and pepper
1 teaspoon dried mixed herbs
1 egg

1 oz. (2 T) margarine
15 oz. can spaghetti in tomato
  sauce
3 oz. (¾ cup) cheese, grated

Mix together the lamb, onion, seasoning, herbs and egg. Form into a
giant burger and chill for 30 minutes. Melt the margarine in a frying
pan (skillet) and fry the burger gently until the underside is brown.
Turn the burger over and cook until brown on the other side. Top
with the canned spaghetti and grated cheese. Cover the pan and cook
until the cheese has melted and the spaghetti is hot. Serve cut into
wedges. This is ideal for cooking over a camping gas stove, or a
barbecue.
**Serves 4-6**

# Wellington Lamb Burgers

4 lamb burgers (see page 19)
1 tablespoon oil
1 tablespoon mint sauce

13 oz. packet frozen puff pastry,
 thawed
1 egg, beaten

Brush the lamb burgers with the oil and grill (broil) for 2-3 minutes on each side. Cool. Spoon over the mint sauce. Roll out the dough and cut out eight fluted circles, larger than the burgers. Place a burger on one circle of dough and brush the edges with egg. Cover with another circle and seal the edges. Enclose the remaining burgers in the same way. From the remaining dough make four strips and place these on top of the dough-covered burgers for decoration.

   Brush with egg and bake in a moderately hot oven, 400°F, Gas Mark 6 for 25-30 minutes or until golden brown. Serve with new potatoes, courgettes (zucchini), tomatoes and onion relish.
**Serves 4**


# Supper-time Burgers

1 onion, chopped
1 oz. (2 T) butter
1 lb. minced (ground) lamb
1 celery stalk, chopped
1 tablespoon tomato purée (paste)

1 tablespoon tomato ketchup
1 teaspoon dried mixed herbs
salt and pepper
2 oz. (1 cup) fresh breadcrumbs
8 soft rolls (buns)

Fry the onion in the butter until softened, then mix with the meat, celery, tomato purée (paste), ketchup, herbs, seasoning and breadcrumbs. Divide into eight portions and shape into burgers. Grill (broil) for 15 minutes until golden and serve in the rolls (buns).
**Makes 8**

WELLINGTON LAMB BURGER
*(Photograph: Crosse & Blackwell)*

# PORK BURGERS

## Sweet and Sour Burgers

1 lb. lean minced (ground) pork
4 oz. (1 cup) flour
salt and pepper
1 egg
oil for frying
**Sweet and sour sauce:**
2 tablespoons cornflour (cornstarch)
3 oz. (6 T) sugar
5 tablespoons vinegar

½ pint (1¼ cups) water
1 tablespoon soy sauce
**Vegetable garnish:**
½ green pepper, cored, seeded and
  cut into strips
½ red pepper, cored, seeded and cut
  into strips
2 carrots, cut into strips
2 slices canned pineapple, cubed

Mix the pork with the flour, seasoning and egg. Divide the mixture into eight and shape into burgers. Heat the oil in a pan and fry the burgers for 10 minutes.

Meanwhile, in a small saucepan mix the cornflour (cornstarch) with the sugar, then stir in the remaining sauce ingredients. Bring to the boil, stirring continuously. Add the vegetable garnish to the sauce and simmer for 10 minutes.

Pour the sauce over the burgers and serve with pasta and salad.
**Serves 4**

# Devilled Pork Burgers

1 lb. pork sausagemeat
1 onion, finely chopped
¼ teaspoon dried sage
salt and pepper
½ oz. (2 T) flour
1 teaspoon dry mustard
1 teaspoon caster sugar

1 teaspoon mild curry powder
1 egg, beaten
2 oz. (½ cup) salted peanuts,
 finely chopped
2 oz. (1 cup) fresh breadcrumbs
oil for frying
4 soft rolls (buns)

Mix together the sausagemeat, onion, sage and seasoning. In a separate bowl, mix together the flour, mustard, sugar and curry powder. Divide the meat mixture into eight portions. Shape into burgers on a board dusted with flour and coat with the seasoned flour. Brush with the beaten egg. Mix together the peanuts and breadcrumbs and use to coat the burgers. Press the coating in well and reshape with a palette knife. Fry the porkburgers in the oil for 8 minutes on each side. Serve in the bread rolls (buns).
**Makes 8**

# Streaky Bacon Burgers

4 soft baps (buns)
4 back bacon rashers (Canadian
 bacon slices)
3 eggs
salt and pepper

1½ tablespoons milk
butter
**Garnish:**
lettuce
tomato slices

Warm the baps (buns). Cut the bacon rashers (slices) in half and grill (broil) until they just begin to crisp and brown. Keep them hot. Beat the eggs with seasoning and milk. Melt a little butter in a small pan and scramble the eggs. Split the baps (buns), spread with butter and fill with the bacon rashers (slices) and scrambled eggs. Add some lettuce and tomato to garnish.
**Serves 4**

# Ham Burgers

6 oz. (¾ cup) minced (ground)
  cooked ham
1 green pepper, cored, seeded and
  finely chopped
1 onion, finely chopped
1 tablespoon finely chopped parsley

salt and pepper
few drops of Worcestershire sauce
1 egg, beaten
2 oz. (¼ cup) margarine
parsley sprigs to garnish

Mix together the ham, green pepper, onion, parsley, seasoning, Worcestershire sauce and egg. Divide into six to eight equal-sized portions and shape into burgers. Melt the margarine in a frying pan (skillet) and gently fry the burgers for 3-4 minutes on each side. Drain on kitchen paper towels and garnish with parsley sprigs.
**Makes 6-8**

# Egg and Ham Burgers

8 oz. (1 cup) cooked ham, finely
  diced
8 oz. (1 cup) mashed potatoes
1 tablespoon chopped parsley

1 egg yolk
4 streaky bacon rashers (slices),
  derinded
4 eggs

Mix together the ham, potatoes, parsley and egg yolk. Divide the mixture into four. Shape into burgers. Wrap a rasher (slice) of bacon around each burger and secure with a wooden cocktail stick. Place the burgers in an ovenproof dish and bake in a moderately hot oven, 375°F, Gas Mark 5 for 20-25 minutes.
  Poach the whole eggs and serve on top of the ham burgers.
**Serves 4**

HAM BURGERS
*(Photograph: Pointerware (U.K.) Limited)*

# Torpedo Burgers

½ oz. (1 T) butter
1 onion, thinly sliced
1 tablespoon Worcestershire sauce
3 tablespoons tomato ketchup

salt and pepper
4 pork sausages
4 long white rolls (hot dog buns)
4 sprigs of watercress to garnish

Melt the butter in a saucepan and fry the onion gently for 10 minutes. Stir in the Worcestershire sauce, ketchup and seasoning and heat through. Grill (broil) the sausages until cooked. Warm the rolls (buns), then split open and place a sausage on the bottom of each. Spoon over the onion mixture and garnish with a sprig of watercress.
**Serves 4**

# Skewered Sausage Burgers

1 lb. pork sausagemeat
4 heaped tablespoons (¼ cup) dry
  sage and onion stuffing mix
salt and pepper
8 button mushrooms
1 red pepper, cored, seeded and cut
  into large chunks
8 bay leaves

4 tablespoons (¼ cup) oil
2 tablespoons beer
12 oz. (1¾ cups) rice
**Sauce:**
14 oz. can tomatoes
1 tablespoon tomato purée (paste)
1 tablespoon Worcestershire sauce
2 teaspoons made mustard

Mix the sausagemeat with the stuffing mix and seasoning. Form into 12 small burgers. Thread onto four skewers with the mushrooms, red pepper chunks and bay leaves. Mix the oil with the beer and brush each kebab. Grill (broil) until golden brown.

Meanwhile, simmer all the sauce ingredients together for 10 minutes. Boil the rice in salted water for 12 minutes. Serve the kebabs with the sauce on a bed of rice.
**Serves 4**

# Double Delicious Burgers

8 oz. (1 cup) lean minced (ground)
 pork
8 oz. (1 cup) pork sausagemeat
3 oz. (½ cup) cooked rice
2 teaspoons dried sage
2 teaspoons English made mustard
salt and pepper

1 egg, beaten
oil for shallow frying
4 bread rolls, halved
few spring onions (scallions),
 shredded
2 tomatoes, sliced
¼ cucumber, sliced

Mix together the minced (ground) pork, sausagemeat, rice, sage,
mustard, seasoning and egg. Divide the mixture into eight portions
then shape into burgers. Heat the oil in a frying pan (skillet) and fry
the burgers for 5 minutes on each side. Arrange four burgers on the
roll bases. Top with spring onions (scallions), tomato and cucumber
slices. Place remaining burgers on top, then cover with the top halves
of the rolls. Serve with storecupboard sauce (see page 76).
**Serves 4**

# Bacon Burgers

1 lb. minced (ground) cooked ham
2 oz. (1 cup) fresh breadcrumbs
1 onion, finely chopped
pinch of dried mixed herbs
salt and pepper
1 egg, beaten
4 streaky bacon rashers (slices)
**Sauce:**
1 oz. (2 T) margarine
1 streaky bacon rasher (slice),
  chopped

1 small onion, sliced
1 small carrot, sliced
1 oz. (¼ cup) flour
¾ pint (2 cups) stock
1 oz. (¼ cup) mushrooms, sliced
4 tablespoons (¼ cup) tomato purée
  (paste)
salt and pepper

To make the sauce, melt the margarine in a saucepan and fry the
bacon, onion and carrot for 1-2 minutes. Stir in the flour and cook
over a low heat until it turns a golden brown. Remove from the heat
and gradually stir in the stock. Add the mushrooms. Bring to the
boil, stirring all the time, and simmer for 20 minutes. Add the
tomato purée (paste) and seasoning and simmer for a further 5
minutes. Strain.

To make the burgers, mix together the ham, breadcrumbs, onion,
mixed herbs and seasoning and bind with egg. Turn onto a floured
board and divide into four. Shape into burgers. Wrap a rasher (slice)
of bacon around each burger and place in an ovenproof dish. Cover
with the sauce. Bake in a moderately hot oven, 375°F, Gas Mark 5
for 40-45 minutes.
**Serves 4**

STREAKY BACON BURGER *(page 31)*
*(Photograph: Danish Food Centre)*

# Bender Bap Burger

8 pork (link) sausages
2 oz. (¼ cup) margarine
1 onion, sliced into rings
4 baps (buns)
1 oz. (2 T) butter

4 canned pineapple rings
4 oz. (1 cup) cheese, grated
4 slices of tomato
4 bacon rolls

Make four cuts in each sausage without cutting completely through. Bend into a semi-circle and secure with a wooden cocktail stick. Fry gently in the melted margarine for 15 minutes. Remove from the pan and keep warm. Fry the onion rings for 5 minutes until softened.

Split each bap (bun) and butter the cut surfaces. Place a pineapple ring, two sausages and some onion rings inside. Sprinkle the cheese on top and grill (broil) until it is melted and golden brown. Top with a slice of tomato and a bacon roll and serve immediately.
**Serves 4**


# Sausage Burgers

1 lb. pork sausagemeat
2 tablespoons Worcestershire sauce
1 onion, grated
2 oz. (1 cup) fresh breadcrumbs

1 egg, beaten
salt and pepper
6 baps (buns)
4 tomatoes, sliced

Mix together the sausagemeat, Worcestershire sauce, onion and breadcrumbs. Add the egg and seasoning and mix well. Shape into six burgers. Cook over a barbecue or grill (broil) for 10-15 minutes, turning once. Toast the cut sides of the baps (buns) on the barbecue or under the grill (broiler). Serve each sausage burger in a toasted bap (bun) topped with sliced tomatoes.
**Serves 6**

# Breakfast Burgers

1 small packet of instant mashed
  potatoes
½ packet dry sage and onion
  stuffing
4 oz. bacon rashers (slices), grilled
  (broiled) and crumbled

2 oz. (¼ cup) butter or margarine
4 eggs
salt and pepper
2 tablespoons milk

Make up the potatoes as directed on the packet. Add the stuffing and
the bacon pieces and mix well. Divide into four and shape into
burgers. Fry in 1 oz. (2T) butter or margarine until crisp and brown.

Beat the eggs with seasoning and milk. Melt the remaining butter
or margarine in a small pan and scramble the eggs. Top each burger
with scrambled egg.
**Serves 4**


# Summer Burgers

4 pork (link) sausages, skinned
flour
salt and pepper
oil and butter
4 hard-boiled eggs
lettuce

4 tablespoons (¼ cup) mayonnaise
**Garnish:**
capers
watercress
lemon wedges

Flatten each skinned sausage into a 'patty'. Coat with flour seasoned
with salt and pepper, and fry on both sides in a mixture of oil and
butter. Allow to cool.

Top each burger with overlapping slices of hard-boiled egg. Serve
on a bed of lettuce with a topping of mayonnaise. Garnish with
capers, watercress and lemon wedges.
**Serves 4**

# Man-sized Burgers

1 ½ lb. minced (ground) pork
4 onions, chopped
4 eggs, beaten
2 tablespoons Worcestershire sauce
salt and pepper

4 oz. (1 cup) cheese, grated
2 garlic cloves, crushed
½ teaspoon Italian seasoning
1 oz. (¼ cup) flour

Mix all the ingredients together. Divide into four big burgers. Grill (broil) for 10 minutes on each side. Serve with salad.
**Serves 4**

# Saucy Burgers

½ oz. (1 T) margarine
½ oz. (2 T) flour
¼ pint (⅔ cup) milk
salt and pepper
2 oz. (½ cup) cheese, grated
4 slices of bread

1 lb. cooked ham, finely chopped
2 oz. (1 cup) fresh breadcrumbs
1 egg
4 canned peach halves
chopped parsley to garnish

Melt the margarine in a saucepan and stir in the flour. Gradually stir in the milk and add seasoning. Stirring all the time, bring to the boil and cook for 2-3 minutes or until thickened and smooth. Remove from the heat and stir in the cheese. Keep warm.
Toast the bread. Mix together the ham, breadcrumbs and egg and form into four burgers. Grill (broil) for 4 minutes on each side. Place a burger on each piece of toast, top with a peach half and pour over the cheese sauce. Grill (broil) for a few minutes longer or until the sauce is bubbly and golden brown. Garnish with parsley.
**Serves 4**

MAN-SIZED BURGERS
*(Photograph: Farmer's Wife News and Views)*

# Giant Potato Burger

*12 oz. back bacon rashers*
*(Canadian bacon slices), diced*
*1 oz. (2T) lard*
*1 egg, separated*

*12 oz. (1½ cups) mashed potatoes*
*salt and pepper*
*3 pork (link) sausages*
*parsley sprig to garnish*

Fry the bacon in a frying pan (skillet), adding the lard if necessary. Beat the egg yolk into the potatoes. Add the chopped bacon and seasoning. Beat the egg white until stiff and fold into the potato mixture. Spread over the bottom of the frying pan (skillet) and cook for 5 minutes or until the mixture is hot and golden brown.

Meanwhile, grill (broil) the sausages.

Turn the potato burger onto a hot serving dish, keeping the golden crust uppermost. Split the sausages in half lengthways and arrange in a wheel on top of the potato burger. Garnish with the sprig of parsley.

**Serves 4-6**

# CHICKEN BURGERS

## Saucy Chicken Burgers

1½ lb. minced (ground) chicken
2 oz. (1 cup) fresh breadcrumbs
1 onion, grated
1 egg
salt and pepper
3 tablespoons oil
1 large onion, sliced

4 oz. (1 cup) mushrooms, sliced
¼ oz. (1 T) flour
½ pint (1¼ cups) stock
1 tablespoon tomato purée (paste)
2 oz. (1 cup) noodles, cooked and
  kept hot

Mix together the chicken, half of the breadcrumbs, the grated onion, egg and seasoning. Shape into eight burgers and coat in the remaining breadcrumbs. Fry in the oil for 15 minutes. Transfer to an ovenproof dish and keep warm.

Put the sliced onion, mushrooms, flour, stock and tomato purée (paste) in a saucepan and bring to the boil. Pour over the burgers and bake in a moderate oven, 350°F, Gas Mark 4 for 30 minutes. Just before serving stir in the noodles.
**Serves 4**

# Chicken Deckers

1 medium-sized packet instant
  mashed potatoes
3 oz. (¾ cup) self-raising flour
10½ oz. can condensed chicken
  soup

6 oz. (¾ cup) cooked chicken
  meat, chopped
6 bacon rolls, grilled (broiled)

Make up the instant mashed potatoes according to the instructions
on the packet and cool. Beat in the flour, then roll out on a floured
surface. Cut out 12 rounds. Grease a frying pan (skillet) and fry the
potato rounds until golden brown. Keep warm.

Heat the undiluted soup with the chopped chicken pieces.
Sandwich together the potato rounds with the chicken mixture and
top each with a bacon roll.

**Serves 6**

# Chinese Burgers

1 lb. minced (ground) chicken
4 oz. (1 cup) flour
1 oz. (2 T) butter
1 pint (2½ cups) chicken stock
2 celery stalks, chopped
2 tomatoes, chopped

¼ cucumber, chopped
1 small onion, sliced
1 carrot, sliced
2 tablespoons soy sauce
salt and pepper
8 oz. (4 cups) bean sprouts

Mix together the chicken and flour and form into 16 small burgers.
Melt the butter and fry the burgers until golden brown.

Put the stock, celery, tomatoes, cucumber, onion and carrot in a
saucepan and bring to the boil. Reduce the heat and add the browned
burgers. Cook for a further 15 minutes. Stir in the soy sauce,
seasoning and bean sprouts and simmer for 2 minutes. Serve
immediately.

**Serves 4**

CHICKEN DECKERS
*(Photograph: Canned Food Advisory Service)*

# Oriental Burgers

1 lb. minced (ground) chicken
1 red chilli (chili pepper), seeded
 and chopped
1 onion, chopped
1 teaspoon chopped fresh root
 ginger

1 teaspoon lemon juice
salt and pepper
1 tablespoon soy sauce
3 tablespoons fresh breadcrumbs
1 teaspoon sesame seeds

Mix together all the ingredients and chill in the refrigerator for 2 hours. Shape into eight burgers and grill (broil).
**Serves 4**


# Corn Burgers

12 oz. (1½ cups) mashed potatoes
8 oz. (1½ cups) sweetcorn kernels
2 oz. (½ cup) flour
salt and pepper
2 oz. (¼ cup) butter
4 bananas

lemon juice
12 oz. (1½ cups) chicken meat,
 chopped
8 streaky bacon rashers (slices),
 chopped
4 tomatoes, sliced, to garnish

Mix together the mashed potatoes, sweetcorn kernels, flour and seasoning. Divide into eight portions and form into flat cakes. Fry in the butter in a frying pan (skillet) until golden brown on both sides. Keep warm.

Dip the bananas in the lemon juice to prevent discoloration, then cut in half lengthways. Put the chicken and bacon in the pan and fry for 5-6 minutes. Add the bananas and fry for a further 2-3 minutes. Divide between the corn cakes and garnish with tomato slices.
**Serves 4**

# Herby Chicken Burgers

1 onion, chopped
3 oz. (6 T) butter
1 lb. minced (ground) chicken
2 oz. (1 cup) fresh breadcrumbs
1 tablespoon milk
1 egg, beaten
pinch of dried mixed herbs

pinch of chopped parsley
salt and pepper
¼ oz. (1 T) flour
**Sauce:**
1 oz. (¼ cup) flour
½ pint (1 ¼ cups) milk
salt and pepper

Fry the onion in a little of the butter until softened. Mix with the chicken, breadcrumbs, milk, egg, herbs and seasoning. Shape into eight burgers and coat with the flour. Fry in the remaining butter, then remove from the pan and keep warm.

Add the flour for the sauce to the butter in the pan. Gradually stir in the milk and bring to the boil. Season and serve poured over the burgers.
**Serves 4**

# Picnic Chicken Burgers

1 medium-sized onion, finely
  chopped
1 oz. (2 T) butter
12 oz. (1½ cups) minced (ground)
  chicken
2 oz. (1 cup) fresh white
  breadcrumbs

salt and pepper
large pinch of dried mixed herbs
1 teaspoon tomato purée (paste)
1 small egg, beaten
1 oz. (¼ cup) seasoned flour
oil for shallow frying

Sauté the onion in the butter until golden brown. Stir in the chicken, breadcrumbs, seasoning, herbs and tomato purée (paste). Bind the mixture with the beaten egg. Divide into four equal portions and shape into round flat cakes. Coat well with the seasoned flour.

Heat the oil in a frying pan (skillet) and fry the burgers for 4-5 minutes each side. Cool and chill then wrap in foil to take on a picnic. Serve with crisp lettuce, a potato salad and a tomato and onion salad.
**Serves 4**


# Eastern Burgers

1 lb. (2 cups) chicken meat,
  chopped
1 onion, chopped
1 garlic clove
2 teaspoons chopped fresh root
  ginger

2 tablespoons lemon juice
1 teaspoon ground coriander
½ teaspoon ground cumin
3 tablespoons plain yogurt
salt and pepper
3 tablespoons fresh breadcrumbs

Place all the ingredients in a liquidizer and blend until smooth. Cover and chill in the refrigerator for 2 hours. Shape into eight burgers and grill (broil) for 8-10 minutes.
**Serves 4**

PICNIC CHICKEN BURGERS
*(Photograph: Buxted Advisory Service and Bacofoil Limited)*

# Chicken Burgers with Spicy Sauce

2 ¼ lb. minced (ground) chicken
1 teaspoon salt
½ teaspoon pepper
1 onion, grated

**Sauce:**
2 tablespoons soy sauce
4 tablespoons (¼ cup) tomato
  ketchup
½ teaspoon dry mustard
1 tablespoon honey
2 teaspoons lemon juice
2 tablespoons water

Mix together the chicken, seasoning and onion and shape into eight burgers. Put all the sauce ingredients in a saucepan and bring to the boil. Brush the burgers with the sauce and grill (broil) for 6–8 minutes. Serve the remaining sauce separately.
**Serves 8**

# Chunky Burgers

4 crusty rolls (buns)
1 teaspoon made mustard
salt and pepper
8 oz. (1 cup) cooked chicken, cut
  into chunks

1 tablespoon mayonnaise
1 tomato, sliced

Split the rolls (buns) in half and spread with the mustard and
seasoning. Divide the chicken between the rolls (buns). Spoon over
the mayonnaise and top each with a tomato slice. Replace the bread
'lids' and heat in a hot oven, 425°F, Gas Mark 7 for 10 minutes.
**Serves 4**

# Mushroom Burgers

½ oz. (1 T) butter
1 onion, chopped
8 oz. (1 cup) minced (ground)
  chicken
1 small can condensed tomato soup

6 oz. (1½ cups) mushrooms, sliced
salt and pepper
¼ teaspoon dry mustard
6 oz. (1½ cups) cheese, grated
3 soft rolls (buns)

Melt the butter and fry the onion until tender. Add the chicken,
soup, mushrooms, seasoning and mustard and simmer for 10
minutes. Remove from the heat and stir in one-third of the cheese
until melted. Split the rolls (buns) in half and toast the cut sides.
Spoon the meat mixture onto the rolls (buns) and grill (broil) for 5
minutes. Sprinkle over the remaining cheese and continue cooking
until the cheese is golden brown.
**Makes 6**

# Golden Burgers

2 oz. (¼ cup) margarine
2 oz. (½ cup) flour
½ pint (1 ¼ cups) milk
salt and pepper
paprika
8 oz. (1 cup) minced (ground)
  chicken

1 tablespoon chopped parsley
1 egg, beaten
2 tablespoons breadcrumbs
oil for deep frying

Place the margarine, flour, milk and seasoning in a saucepan and, stirring continuously, bring to the boil. Cook for 2-3 minutes. Cool, then stir in the chicken and parsley. Shape into eight burgers. Coat with the egg and breadcrumbs and deep fry for 5 minutes until golden. Serve with granary (wholewheat) rolls (buns).
**Serves 4**


# Burgundy Burgers

8 oz. (1 cup) minced (ground)
  chicken
8 oz. onions, chopped
¼ pint (⅔ cup) burgundy wine
1 egg, beaten

2 oz. (2 cups) cornflakes, crushed
salt and pepper
1 tablespoon oil
4 fried eggs, hot
4 soft rolls (buns)

Mix together the meat, onions, wine, egg, cornflakes and seasoning. Divide into four portions and shape into burgers. Fry in the hot oil for 4-5 minutes on each side. Top each burger with a fried egg and serve in a roll (bun) with salad.
**Serves 4**

KIPPER BURGERS *(page 55)*
*(Photograph: Mazola)*

# Skewered Chicken Burgers

1 lb. minced (ground) chicken
3 tablespoons fresh breadcrumbs
salt and pepper
1 garlic clove, crushed
1 egg
1 tablespoon chopped parsley

8 bacon rashers (slices)
2 pears, cored and sliced
4 courgettes (zucchini), sliced
1 tablespoon oil

Mix together the chicken, breadcrumbs, seasoning, garlic, egg and parsley. Shape into 16 small burgers. Cut the bacon into pieces. Thread the burgers, bacon, pears, and courgettes (zucchini) onto skewers. Brush with the oil and grill (broil) until cooked through.
**Serves 4**

# Basil Burgers

1 lb. minced (ground) chicken
1 tablespoon chopped fresh basil
1 teaspoon lemon juice
salt and pepper

½ oz. (¼ cup) fresh breadcrumbs
4 tablespoons (¼ cup) oil
1 onion, sliced
1 tomato, sliced

Mix together the chicken, basil, lemon juice, seasoning and breadcrumbs. Shape into eight burgers. Brush with half the oil and grill (broil) for 5–8 minutes. Fry the onion and tomato slices in the remaining oil and divide between the burgers.
**Serves 4**

# FISH BURGERS

## Crunchy Burgers

4 oz. salmon, cooked and flaked
1 oz. (¼ cup) fresh breadcrumbs
1 celery stalk, chopped
1 teaspoon grated onion
salt and pepper

1 teaspoon anchovy essence
 (¼ T anchovy paste)
1 tablespoon chopped parsley
pinch of paprika pepper

Mix all the ingredients together and shape into four burgers. Serve with a crunchy walnut salad.
**Serves 4**

## Kipper Burgers

1 lb. (2 cups) mashed potatoes
14 oz. kipper fillets, cooked and
 flaked
2 hard-boiled eggs, chopped
2 tablespoons chopped parsley
salt and black pepper

dash of Tabasco sauce
1 teaspoon lemon juice
2 eggs
½ oz. (2 T) flour
1 oz. (¼ cup) dry breadcrumbs
oil for frying

Mix together the potatoes, fish, hard-boiled eggs, parsley, seasoning, Tabasco, lemon juice and one egg. Form into four large or eight small burgers. Roll in the flour, then dip in the remaining egg and coat in the breadcrumbs. Deep fry until golden brown and crisp. Drain on kitchen paper towels and serve hot.
**Serves 4**

# Fish Burgers

8 oz. (1 cup) mashed potatoes
1 oz. (2 T) margarine
salt and pepper
8 oz. fish fillets, cooked and flaked
1 tablespoon chopped parsley

1 teaspoon lemon juice
1 small egg
golden breadcrumbs
oil for deep frying

Mix together the potatoes, margarine, seasoning, fish, parsley and lemon juice. Turn onto a floured surface and divide into eight portions. Shape into burgers. Coat with egg and breadcrumbs and deep fry in the oil. Drain well before serving.
**Makes 8**

# Deep Sea Burgers

4 oz. cod fillet, cooked and flaked
6 oz. (¾ cup) mashed potatoes
2 oz. (½ cup) flour

1 teaspoon dried mixed herbs
salt and pepper
2 oz. (¼ cup) butter

Mix together the fish, potatoes, flour, herbs and seasoning. Divide into eight and shape into burgers on a floured surface. Fry in the butter until golden brown on both sides.
**Serves 4**

# Neptune Burgers

1 lb. potatoes, grated
1 lb. smoked haddock fillets, finely
   chopped
1 egg, beaten
1 teaspoon anchovy essence
   (¼ T anchovy paste)

salt and pepper
lemon juice
1 teaspoon oil
6-8 bread rolls (buns), split

Squeeze the potatoes in a cloth to remove excess moisture. Mix the potatoes with the fish, egg, anchovy essence (paste), seasoning and lemon juice and shape into six to eight burgers. Brush with the oil and arrange on a baking sheet. Bake in a moderate oven, 350°F, Gas Mark 4 for 30 minutes, turning the burgers over halfway through cooking. Serve in the rolls (buns) with chutney.
**Serves 6-8**


# Party Burgers

7 oz. can salmon, drained and
   mashed
8 oz. (1 cup) mashed potatoes
1 tablespoon ketchup
pinch of cayenne pepper
1 oz. (¼ cup) flour
1 egg, beaten
4 oz. (1 cup) toasted breadcrumbs
oil for frying

**Sauce:**
2 tablespoons mayonnaise
1 tablespoon tomato chutney
2 tablespoons chopped chives
1 canned pimiento, chopped
½ small green pepper, cored, seeded
   and chopped
1 teaspoon paprika

Mix the salmon with the potatoes, ketchup and cayenne and shape into mini-burgers. Coat in the flour, then egg and crumb. Fry in the hot oil until golden. Allow to cool on kitchen paper towels.

   Mix all the sauce ingredients together and chill. Serve the burgers with cocktail sticks so that they can be dunked in the sauce.
**Note:** The burgers may also be served hot.
**Serves 6-8**

# Mini Burgers in Spicy Sauce

2 oz. (¼ cup) long-grain rice
7 oz. can tuna fish, drained and
 flaked
8 oz. can pineapple chunks,
 drained and chopped
1 teaspoon mayonnaise
1 teaspoon tomato purée (paste)
salt and pepper
1 tablespoon chopped cucumber
1 egg
2 oz. (⅔ cup) golden breadcrumbs
oil for frying

1 green pepper, cored, seeded and
 cut into rings, to garnish
**Sauce:**
2 tablespoons tomato ketchup
2 teaspoons vinegar
2 teaspoons sugar
pineapple can syrup made up to
 ½ pint (1¼ cups) with water
1 tablespoon cornflour (cornstarch),
 mixed to a paste with a little
 water

Cook the rice in boiling salted water for 10-15 minutes. Drain if
necessary and keep warm. Mix together the tuna, pineapple chunks,
mayonnaise, tomato purée (paste), seasoning, cucumber and the rice.
Bind together with the egg. Divide into 12 and shape into burgers.
Coat with the breadcrumbs and fry in the hot oil for 3-4 minutes.

 Meanwhile, put all the sauce ingredients into a saucepan and bring
to the boil, stirring continuously. Simmer until thick and smooth.
Pour the sauce over the cooked burgers and garnish with the pepper
rings.
**Serves 4-6**

# Sea Burgers

1 lb. (2 cups) mashed potatoes
½ oz. (2 T) flour
salt and pepper
2 oz. (¼ cup) butter
8 oz. kipper fillets, cooked and
  flaked

2 hard-boiled eggs, chopped
2 tablespoons mayonnaise
2 teaspoons vinegar
cayenne pepper
celery salt

Mix together the potatoes, flour and seasoning. Roll out on a floured surface to about ½ inch thick. Cut into eight rounds with a pastry (cookie) cutter. Fry in the butter until lightly browned on both sides.

Combine the fish, eggs, mayonnaise, vinegar, cayenne and celery salt. Sandwich the potato cakes together with the fish mixture.
**Serves 4**


# Savoury Rounds

3 flat rolls (buns)
1 onion, finely chopped
1 tablespoon oil
8 oz. can tuna fish, drained and
  flaked
8 oz. can tomatoes, drained

juice of 1 lemon
2 teaspoons dried mixed herbs
salt and pepper
1 egg
4 oz. (1 cup) cheese, grated

Slice the rolls (buns) in half and scoop out a little of the dough. Fry the onion in the oil until golden. Add the fish, tomatoes, lemon juice, herbs, seasoning and egg. Pile onto the rolls (buns) and sprinkle over the cheese. Cook under the grill (broiler) for 5 minutes. Serve hot.
**Serves 3**

SEA BURGERS
*(Photograph: White Fish Kitchen)*

# Mackerel Burgers

12 oz. smoked mackerel fillets,
 flaked
3 oz. (1½ cups) fresh breadcrumbs
salt and pepper
3 oz. (¾ cup) celery, chopped
grated rind of ½ lemon

1 egg, beaten
4 rolls (buns)
2 radishes, sliced
mayonnaise
4 sprigs of watercress to garnish

Mix together the mackerel, breadcrumbs, seasoning, celery, lemon
rind and egg. Shape into four burgers and grill (broil) until golden.
Split the rolls (buns) and fill each with a burger, slices of radish and a
spoonful of mayonnaise. Serve garnished with watercress.
**Serves 4**

# Pilchard Burgers

1 large packet instant mashed
  potatoes
1 medium-sized can pilchards,
  drained and flaked
3 oz. (½ cup) sweetcorn kernels

2 tablespoons chopped lemon balm
salt and pepper
beaten egg
dry breadcrumbs
oil for frying

Make up the potatoes according to the instructions on the packet.
Stir in the pilchards, sweetcorn, lemon balm and seasoning. Turn
onto a floured surface and shape into eight burgers. Dip in beaten
egg, then coat in breadcrumbs. Fry in the hot oil until golden. Serve
with tomato sauce.
**Serves 4**

# Smoky Burgers

1 lb. (2 cups) mashed potatoes
12 oz. smoked haddock fillets,
  cooked and flaked
1 hard-boiled egg, chopped
3 tablespoons powdered milk
salt and pepper

2 tablespoons chopped parsley
½ teaspoon dry mustard
1 egg, beaten
browned breadcrumbs
2 oz. (¼ cup) butter
8 brown rolls (buns), split

Mix together the potatoes, fish, egg, milk, seasoning, parsley and
mustard. Shape into eight burgers. Brush with the beaten egg and
coat with breadcrumbs. Fry on both sides in the butter until golden
brown. Drain well and serve in the rolls (buns) with salad.
**Makes 8**

# Dab Burgers

8 small dab fillets
salt and black pepper
2 oz. (¼ cup) butter
8 bacon rashers (slices)

8 thin slices of cheese
4 crusty bread rolls (buns)
4 large tomatoes, sliced
4 sprigs of watercress to garnish

Season the fillets with salt and pepper and dot with the butter. Grill (broil) the fish and bacon for 3–4 minutes. After 2 minutes, lay a slice of cheese on each fish fillet and continue grilling (broiling) until the cheese has melted. Cut each roll (bun) into three slices and layer the fish, bacon and tomatoes with the bread. Serve garnished with watercress.
**Serves 4**


# Trawler Burgers

4 oz (½ cup) mashed potatoes
4 oz. (1 cup) self-raising flour
1 oz. (2 T) butter, melted
salt
1 tablespoon milk

8 oz. tomatoes, sliced
1 onion, chopped
4 oz. (1 cup) cheese, grated
2 oz. (½ cup) mushrooms, sliced
12 oz. cod fillets, finely chopped

Mix together the potatoes, flour, butter and salt. Add the milk and more flour if necessary to form a stiff dough. Divide into four and shape into large rounds. Grill (broil) until golden on both sides.

Mix together the remaining ingredients and pile on top of the potato rounds. Return to the heat and grill (broil) for a further 10 minutes.
**Serves 4**

DAB BURGER
*(Photograph: White Fish Kitchen)*

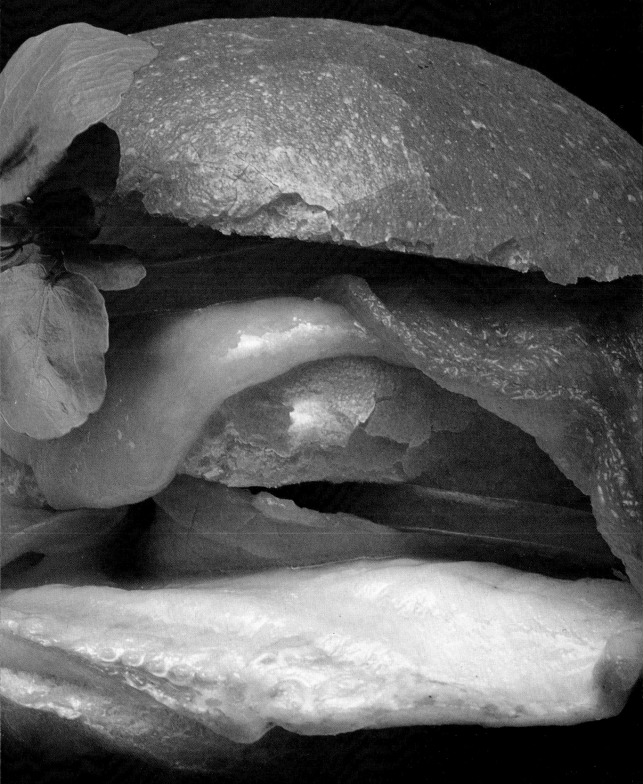

# TOASTED SANDWICHES

## Curried Ham and Cheese Toasty

*8 slices of white bread*
*3 oz. (6 T) butter*
*4 slices of cheese*

*4 slices of cooked ham*
*1 banana, sliced*
*pinch of curry powder*

Spread the bread with the butter. Layer the cheese, ham and banana on 4 slices and sprinkle over the curry powder. Top with the remaining bread slices and grill (broil) until golden brown and serve hot.
**Serves 4**

## Toasted Beef

*8 slices of bread*
*3 oz. (6 T) butter*
*8 slices of cold cooked beef*

*1 tablespoon horseradish sauce*
*1 tomato, sliced*
*4 slices of cheese*

Spread the bread with the butter. Layer the beef, horseradish sauce, tomato and cheese on 4 slices. Top with the remaining bread slices and grill (broil) until golden brown. Serve hot.
**Serves 4**

# Cheddar Toasty

8 slices of brown bread
3 oz. (6 T) butter
4 oz. (1 cup) cheese, grated

pinch of garlic salt
1 onion, finely chopped
1 tablespoon sweet pickle (relish)

Toast the bread under the grill (broiler) on one side only. Beat together the butter, cheese, garlic salt, onion and pickle (relish). Use to sandwich together the toasted sides of the bread. Grill (broil) until golden brown and serve hot.
**Serves 4**

# Pineapple Surprise

8 slices of brown bread
3 oz. (6 T) butter
4 oz. (½ cup) cream cheese

pineapple pieces
chopped chives
lemon juice

Spread the bread with the butter. Sandwich the slices together with cream cheese and pineapple pieces sprinkled with chives and lemon juice. Grill (broil) until golden brown and serve hot.
**Serves 4**

# Crusty Mushroom Loaf

1 small crusty loaf
1 oz. (2 T) butter
1 tablespoon flour
½ pint (1¼ cups) milk

salt and pepper
4 oz. (1 cup) mushrooms, sliced
1 tablespoon chopped parsley
2 hard-boiled eggs, chopped

Remove the top from the loaf and scoop out the centre. Bake in a moderate oven, 350°F, Gas Mark 4 until crisp inside. Melt the butter in a saucepan and stir in the flour. Gradually stir in the milk and add seasoning. Bring to the boil over a gentle heat, stirring continuously. Cook for 2–3 minutes until thickened and smooth. Stir in the mushrooms, parsley and eggs. Fill the bread shell with the mixture and replace the top. Return to the oven to bake for 10 minutes. Slice and serve hot with salad.
**Serves 4**


# Peppered Pâté Sandwich

8 slices of granary (wholewheat)
  bread
3 oz. (6 T) margarine
4 oz. coarse pâté

salt and pepper
2 tablespoons finely chopped green
  pepper

Spread the bread with the margarine, then spread four slices with pâté. Sprinkle with seasoning and the green pepper and place the other bread slices on top to make sandwiches. Grill (broil) until golden brown on both sides and serve hot.
**Serves 4**


# Cheese Dreams

4 oz. (1 cup) cheese, grated
1 tablespoon rosehip syrup
1 teaspoon French mustard

salt and pepper
6 slices of white bread
2 oz. (¼ cup) butter

Mix the grated cheese with the rosehip syrup, mustard and seasoning. Spread evenly over three slices of bread. Cover with the remaining slices of bread to form sandwiches. Melt the butter in a frying-pan (skillet) and fry the sandwiches until brown and crisp on both sides. Cut each into four and serve piping hot.
**Serves 3**

CRUSTY MUSHROOM LOAF
*(Photograph: Mushroom Growers' Association)*

# Sardine Savouries

8 slices of granary (wholewheat)
  bread
3 oz. (6T) butter
1 teaspoon capers, chopped

8 canned sardines in tomato sauce
chopped cucumber
celery salt

Spread the bread with the butter. Mash together the capers, sardines, cucumber and celery salt. Spread onto the buttered bread and grill (broil) until golden brown. Serve hot.
**Serves 4**

# Toasted Tuna

4 slices of wholewheat bread
2 oz. (¼ cup) butter
1 small can tuna fish, drained and
  flaked

few drops of lemon juice
2 tablespoons mayonnaise
2 tablespoons chopped cucumber

Toast the bread under the grill (broiler) on one side only. Spread two of the toasted sides with the butter. Mix together the fish, lemon juice, mayonnaise and cucumber and divide between the two slices. Top with the remaining bread and grill (broil) untoasted sides. Serve hot.
**Serves 2**

# Thousand Island Sandwiches

2 hard-boiled eggs, chopped
4 oz. (1 cup) Gruyère cheese,
  grated
7 oz. can tuna fish, drained and
  flaked
5 sweet pickled onions, chopped

4 tablespoons (¼ cup) thousand
  island dressing (see page 80)
salt and pepper
1½ oz. (3 T) butter
12 large slices of white bread

Place the egg, cheese, tuna, pickled onions, dressing, salt and pepper
in a bowl and mix thoroughly.

Melt the butter in a small pan and brush it onto one side of each of
the slices of bread. Place 6 of the slices, butter side down, on a board.
Spread each with some of the filling, and top with another slice of
bread, butter side up. Grill (broil) on both sides until golden. Cut in
half to serve.
**Serves 4–6**


# Double-decker Sandwich

4 slices wholemeal (wholewheat)
  bread
4 slices white bread
butter or margarine
12 thin slices processed cheese

12 thin slices ham
**Garnish:**
1 tomato, sliced
watercress sprigs

Toast the bread and spread with butter or margarine. Place the 4
slices of white bread on a board and arrange 2 slices of cheese and 2
slices of ham on each. Top with the wholemeal (wholewheat) slices
of bread.

Cut the remaining 4 slices of cheese and 4 slices of ham in half to
give 8 triangles of each. Fold each triangle to a horn shape and
arrange 2 cheese horns and 2 ham horns on top of each sandwich.
Garnish with tomato slices and watercress. Transfer to plate and
serve immediately.
**Serves 4**

# SAUCES AND DRESSINGS

## Barbecue Sauce

1 tablespoon cooking oil
2 onions, chopped
1 streaky bacon rasher (slice),
  chopped
1 tablespoon tomato purée (paste)
½ pint (1¼ cups) cider (hard cider)
2 oz. (⅓ cup) demerara (raw)
  sugar

1 tablespoon Worcestershire sauce
1 tablespoon sweet chutney
salt and pepper
1 teaspoon arrowroot
2 tablespoons water

Heat the oil in a saucepan and fry the onions and bacon until transparent. Add the remaining ingredients, except the arrowroot and water. Bring to the boil and simmer for 20 minutes. Remove from the heat. Dissolve the arrowroot in the water and add to the sauce. Return to the heat and bring to the boil, stirring. Cook for a further 1-2 minutes and serve.

BARBECUE SAUCE
*(Photograph: Mazola)*

# Spicy Sauce

1 oz. (2 T) margarine
1 onion, chopped
1 garlic clove, crushed
3 tablespoons lemon juice
3 tablespoons Worcestershire sauce

3 tablespoons tomato purée (paste)
1 teaspoon curry powder
1 stock (bouillon) cube
½ pint (1¼ cups) water
½ teaspoon dried sage

Melt the margarine and fry the onion and garlic for 3–4 minutes. Add the remaining ingredients and bring to the boil. Simmer for 20 minutes.

# Cumberland Sauce

1 orange
1 lemon
4 tablespoons (¼ cup) redcurrant
 jelly

¼ teaspoon dry mustard
pinch of ground ginger
pinch of black pepper

Pare half the rind from the orange and lemon and cut into very thin strips. Place in a bowl, cover with boiling water and blanch for 5 minutes. Drain well. Squeeze the juice from the fruit. Heat the redcurrant jelly in a small saucepan with the drained orange and lemon rind and juices, mustard, ginger and pepper. Adjust the seasoning and serve.

# Lemon Mint Sauce

6 oz. (½ cup) honey
6 fl. oz. (¾ cup) lemon juice
4 tablespoons (¼ cup) water

2 tablespoons chopped fresh mint
1 teaspoon melted butter

Combine the honey, lemon juice and water in a saucepan. Heat gently for 2-3 minutes. Stir in the mint and the melted butter.

# Tomato Sauce

14 oz. can tomatoes
1 oz. (2 T) margarine
1 oz. (¼ cup) flour

1 tablespoon tomato purée (paste)
1 bay leaf
salt and pepper

Sieve (strain) the can of tomatoes and make up to ½ pint (1¼ cups) with water. Put all the ingredients in a saucepan and, stirring continuously over a moderate heat, bring to the boil. Reduce the heat and simmer, covered, for 10 minutes. Remove the bay leaf and serve.

# Storecupboard Sauce

1 tablespoon cornflour (cornstarch)
1 tablespoon dry mustard
½ pint (1 ¼ cups) water
4 tablespoons tomato ketchup

4 tablespoons bottled brown sauce
pinch of paprika
2 oz. (⅓ cup) demerara (raw)
 sugar

Place the cornflour (cornstarch) and mustard in a small pan and gradually blend in the water. Add the remaining ingredients, and bring to the boil, stirring. Simmer for a few minutes, stirring occasionally, then serve.

# Brown Sauce

1 oz. (2 T) margarine
1 oz. (¼ cup) flour
1 small carrot, sliced

1 small onion, sliced
¾ pint (2 cups) stock
salt and pepper

Put the margarine, flour and vegetables in a saucepan and fry gently for 5-10 minutes. Add the stock and seasoning and bring to the boil, stirring continuously. Cover and simmer for 30 minutes, stirring occasionally. Strain and season to taste.

# Yogurt Dressing

¼ pint (⅔ cup) plain yogurt
1 tablespoon chopped chives
1 teaspoon lemon juice

¼ teaspoon dry mustard
salt and pepper

Mix all the ingredients together and chill before serving.

DOUBLE DELICIOUS BURGER (page 35) with
STORECUPBOARD SAUCE (Photograph: Hammonds Sauces)

# Mayonnaise

2 egg yolks
½ teaspoon dry mustard
½ teaspoon salt
¼ teaspoon pepper

½ pint (1¼ cups) olive oil
2 tablespoons wine vinegar or
   lemon juice

If possible have all the ingredients at room temperature, as eggs taken straight from the refrigerator tend to curdle.

Place the egg yolks in a bowl and beat with the mustard, salt and pepper until they become creamy in colour. Gradually beat in half the oil, drop by drop, until the sauce is thick and shiny. Beat in half the vinegar or lemon juice, then beat in the remaining oil, a little more quickly. Beat in the remaining vinegar or lemon juice. If you wish to thin the mayonnaise down a little, add some lemon juice, a little single (light) cream or 1-2 tablespoons hot water.

Thick mayonnaise may be stored in an airtight container in the refrigerator for about two weeks.
**Note:** If the mayonnaise does curdle, beat another egg yolk in a clean bowl and beat in the curdled mixture a teaspoon at a time.

# Green Goddess Dressing

8 fl. oz. (1 cup) mayonnaise (see
   above)
2 anchovy fillets, chopped
2 spring onions (scallions), chopped
1 tablespoon chopped fresh parsley

1 teaspoon chopped fresh thyme
2 teaspoons wine vinegar
4 fl. oz. (½ cup) sour or double
   (heavy) cream
salt and pepper

Pour the mayonnaise into a serving bowl and gradually beat in all the remaining ingredients, adding salt and pepper to taste. Chill in the refrigerator for 30 minutes before serving.

# Sunflower Mayonnaise

½ teaspoon sugar
1 teaspoon dry mustard
½ teaspoon salt
pinch of cayenne pepper

4 tablespoons (¼ cup) lemon juice
1 egg white
14 fl. oz. (1¾ cups) sunflower
  seed oil

Put the sugar, mustard and seasoning in a small bowl and mix with 1
teaspoon of the lemon juice. Beat the egg white until stiff. Add half
the oil to the egg white, a little at a time, beating well after each
addition. Continue beating and gradually add the lemon juice
mixture. Add the remaining oil gradually and then the remaining
lemon juice.

# French Dressing

4 fl. oz. (½ cup) olive oil
4 tablespoons (¼ cup) wine
  vinegar
¼ teaspoon dry mustard

1 garlic clove, crushed (optional)
½ teaspoon sugar
salt and pepper

Put all the ingredients into a screw-topped jar and shake well until
thoroughly blended. This will keep for several weeks. Always shake
well before using.

# Thousand Island Dressing

12 fl. oz. (1½ cups) mayonnaise
  (see page 78)
1 teaspoon Tabasco sauce
2 tablespoons sweet pickle

2 hard-boiled eggs, chopped
2 spring onions (scallions), chopped
3 tablespoons French dressing (see
  above)

Place all the ingredients in a bowl and beat well until thoroughly
blended. Chill in the refrigerator before serving.

# Blue Cheese Dressing

2 oz. blue cheese, such as Danish
  Blue

¼ pint (⅔ cup) plain yogurt
salt and pepper

Rub the cheese through a sieve (strainer) and mix with the yogurt.
Season to taste with salt and pepper. Chill in the refrigerator before
serving.

DOUBLE DECKER SANDWICH (page 71)
(Photograph: Outline Slimming Bureau)

# SALADS

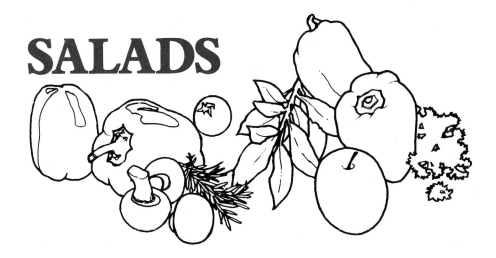

## Tomato Spaghetti Salad

1 medium-sized can spaghetti in
   tomato sauce
6 tablespoons oil and vinegar
   dressing
salt and pepper
3 celery stalks, chopped
1 green pepper, cored, seeded and
   cut into strips

1 onion, finely chopped
1 oz. (¼ cup) unsalted peanuts,
   chopped
lettuce leaves
croûtons

Put the spaghetti in a saucepan and heat with half the oil and vinegar
dressing until the dressing has been absorbed by the pasta. Remove
from the heat and cool. Place in a bowl and toss with the remaining
ingredients.
**Serves 4–6**

## Orange Salad

8 oz. cheese, cubed
3 oranges, segmented
1 head of chicory (French or
   Belgian endive), chopped

1 green pepper, cored, seeded and
   cut into rings
¼ pint (⅔ cup) oil and vinegar
   dressing

Mix together the cheese, oranges, chicory (endive) and green pepper
and toss in the oil and vinegar dressing just before serving.
**Serves 4**

# French Salad

1 garlic clove, halved
sliced cucumber
lettuce leaves
watercress

sliced tomatoes
chopped fresh lemon balm
oil and vinegar dressing

Rub the inside of a salad bowl with the cut sides of the garlic clove.
Discard the garlic. Add the salad ingredients and toss in the oil and
vinegar dressing.

# Winter Salad

1 small red cabbage, cored and
  shredded
1 small cauliflower, broken into
  florets
1 onion, chopped
2 carrots, grated

**Mustard and cheese dressing:**
2 teaspoons French mustard
6 tablespoons oil
2 tablespoons vinegar
juice of ½ orange
2 oz. blue cheese, crumbled
salt and pepper

Mix all the vegetables together. Combine all the dressing ingredients,
add to the vegetables and toss well to coat.
**Serves 4-6**

# Oriental Pasta Salad

6 oz. pasta shapes
salt
6 oz. (3 cups) bean sprouts
2 carrots, grated
½ cucumber, sliced
1 small can pineapple chunks,
  drained

**Dressing:**
6 tablespoons oil
2 tablespoons orange juice
2 tablespoons pineapple can syrup
1 tablespoon soy sauce
pinch of ground ginger

Cook the pasta shapes in boiling, salted water until just tender.
Meanwhile, mix all the dressing ingredients together. Drain the pasta
and while it is still warm mix with the dressing. Allow to cool. Add
the bean sprouts, carrots, cucumber and pineapple and toss lightly
together.
**Serves 4-6**


# Bean Salad

14 oz. can red kidney beans,
  drained
4 oz. (½ cup) cooked green beans,
  sliced
½ head of celery, cut into
  matchsticks

½ cucumber, diced
10 black olives
¼ pint (⅔ cup) oil and vinegar
  dressing

Toss the vegetables with the oil and vinegar dressing. Allow to
marinate for at least 30 minutes before serving.
**Serves 4-6**

ORIENTAL PASTA SALAD, BEAN SALAD
*(Photograph: Canned Food Advisory Service)*

# Rice Salad

4 oz. (³/4 cup) rice, cooked
1 red eating apple, peeled, cored
 and diced
2 celery stalks, chopped
4 oz. (1 cup) mushrooms, sliced
2 tablespoons sultanas (seedless
 white raisins)

4 spring onions (scallions), chopped
1 garlic clove, crushed
1 tablespoon chopped parsley
salt and pepper
¼ pint (²/3 cup) oil and vinegar
 dressing

Mix together the rice, apple, celery, mushrooms, sultanas (raisins),
spring onions (scallions), garlic, parsley and seasoning. Toss in oil
and vinegar dressing to taste.
**Serves 4**

# Spinach and Mushroom Salad

8 oz. spinach, washed and dried
12 oz. (3 cups) button mushrooms,
 finely sliced
2 spring onions (scallions), finely
 chopped
1 tablespoon chopped fresh parsley
 to garnish

**Dressing:**
4 tablespoons (¼ cup) olive oil
1 tablespoon tarragon vinegar
1 tablespoon lemon juice
1 garlic clove, crushed
salt and pepper

Tear the spinach leaves and put them in a salad bowl. Add the
mushrooms and spring onions (scallions) and mix well. Mix all the
dressing ingredients together. Pour over the spinach mixture and toss
well to coat. Sprinkle over the parsley before serving.
**Serves 4**

# Coleslaw Salad

½ white cabbage, cored and finely
  chopped
1 carrot, grated
1 celery stalk, chopped
1 onion, chopped
1 red eating apple, cored and sliced

¼ green pepper, cored, seeded and
  chopped
2 tablespoons raisins
1 oz. (¼ cup) walnuts, chopped
¼ pint (⅔ cup) mayonnaise

Mix all the salad ingredients together. Add the mayonnaise and toss
well to coat.
**Serves 4-6**

# Spinach and Bacon Salad

8 oz. spinach, washed and dried
1 large potato, cooked and diced
2 oz. (¾ cup) Gruyère cheese,
  diced
4 streaky bacon rashers (slices)

5 tablespoons (⅓ cup) oil and
  vinegar dressing
1 tablespoon chopped fresh parsley
  to garnish

Tear the spinach leaves and put them in a salad bowl. Add the potato and cheese and toss well.

Fry the bacon until crisp then drain on paper towels. Chop or crumble the bacon and add to the salad. Pour over the dressing and toss well to coat. Sprinkle over the parsley before serving.
**Serves 4**

# Maryland Salad

4 oz. (1 cup) macaroni shells
4 oz. (⅔ cup) sweetcorn kernels
1 red pepper, cored, seeded and
  chopped

2 spring onions (scallions), chopped
5 tablespoons (⅓ cup) thousand
  island dressing (see page 80)

Cook the macaroni shells in boiling, salted water for 8–10 minutes or until they are 'al dente' (just tender to the bite). Drain, then rinse in cold water. Put the shells into a salad bowl with the sweetcorn kernels, red pepper and spring onions (scallions) and mix well.

Pour over the dressing and toss well to coat.
**Serves 4–6**

# Crunchy Mixed Salad

1 lb. potatoes, cooked and diced
¼ pint (⅔ cup) mayonnaise
2 oz. (½ cup) walnuts, chopped
1 onion, diced

2 carrots, diced
1 green pepper, seeded and diced
salt and freshly ground pepper
lettuce leaves

Place all the ingredients, except the lettuce, in a bowl and mix well together. Line a serving bowl with lettuce leaves and pile the salad into the centre.
**Serves 4**

# Salad Marguerite

1 small cauliflower, broken into
 florets
8 oz. (2 cups) green beans, sliced
8 oz. potatoes, peeled
10 oz. can asparagus tips, drained

6 fl. oz. (¾ cup) mayonnaise
salt and pepper
¼ teaspoon cayenne pepper
1 lettuce, shredded
4 hard-boiled eggs, thinly sliced

Cook the cauliflower and beans in boiling, salted water for 8-10
minutes, or until they are tender. Meanwhile, cook the potatoes in
boiling, salted water for 15 minutes, or until they are cooked. Drain
the vegetables and leave to cool. Slice the potatoes and place in a
bowl with the cauliflower and beans. Stir in the asparagus tips.

Mix the mayonnaise, salt, pepper and cayenne together, then pour
over the vegetables. Toss well to coat.

Line a salad bowl with the lettuce and spoon the vegetable mixture
into the centre. Remove the egg yolks from the whites. Arrange the
egg whites over the salad to look like flower petals. Finely chop the
yolk and sprinkle into the centre.
**Serves 4-6**

# INDEX

# INDEX

PDO 81-752